Leading in the Spirit

Foundations of Leadership

VOLUME 1

A 31-DAY DEVOTIONAL FOR CHRISTIAN LEADERS

DR. LINDA Y. CURETON

Leading in the Spirit

© 2025 Linda Cureton. All rights reserved. No part of this publication may be reproduced, stored in a retrieval system, or transmitted in any form or by any means—electronic, mechanical, photocopying, recording, or otherwise—without prior written permission from the publisher, except for brief quotations used in reviews or other noncommercial uses permitted by copyright law.

Scripture quotations taken from the Holy Bible, New International Version®, NIV®. Copyright © 1973, 1978, 1984, 2011 by Biblica, Inc.™ Used by permission. All rights reserved worldwide.

Scripture quotations taken from the Holy Bible, New Living Translation (NLT), Copyright © 1996, 2004, 2015 by Tyndale House Foundation. Used by permission of Tyndale House Publishers, Carol Stream, Illinois 60188. All rights reserved.

Scriptures marked ESV are taken from THE HOLY BIBLE, ENGLISH STANDARD VERSION (ESV): Scriptures taken from THE HOLY BIBLE, ENGLISH STANDARD VERSION ® Copyright© 2001 by Crossway, a publishing ministry of Good News Publishers, used by permission.

Scriptures marked KJV are taken from the KING JAMES VERSION (KJV): KING JAMES VERSION, public domain.

Published by:

Muse

Muse Technologies, Inc.
4601 Presidents Drive Suite 240
Lanham, MD 20706

Digital ISBN: 979-8-9929301-5-3

Trade Paperback ISBN: 979-8-9929301-4-6

Hardback ISBN 979-8-9929301-3-9

Table of Contents

Foreword 1

Introduction: Leading in the Spirit 3

Week 1: Foundation and Calling 7
    Day 1: A Leader's Desert Experience 9
    Day 2: Embracing Your Divine Calling 11
    Day 3: Masterpiece: Destined for Greatness 13
    Day 4: Leading Through Transition 15
    Day 5: A Mentor 17
    Day 6: Called Without Talent? 19
    Day 7: Pursue 21

Week 2: Character and Integrity 23
    Day 8: Boots Before Horses 25
    Day 9: Guarding Against Greed 27
    Day 10: The Power of Words 29
    Day 11: Skeletons and the Spirit 31
    Day 12: When God Is Listening 33
    Day 13: Strength in Stillness 35
    Day 14: The Road Less Traveled 37

Week 3: Spiritual Discernment 39
    Day 15: Burning Bush Moments 41
    Day 16: Faith and Works: Vision with Action 43
    Day 17: Becoming the Answer to Prayers 45

Day 18: Found in the Wilderness 47
Day 19: Wait for It—God's Appointed Time 49
Day 20: Embracing God's Non-Linear Pathways 51
Day 21: Nothing Is Random in Divine Order................................ 53

Week 4: Leading Through Adversity 55
Day 22: Alexander the Coppersmith 57
Day 23: Faithfulness in Isolation 59
Day 24: Let God Fight Your Battles 61
Day 25: Power in Vulnerability 63
Day 26: The Judas in the Room 65
Day 27: Our "Jobian" Existence.. 67
Day 28: The Furnace of Character 69

Week 5: Vision and Direction.. 71
Day 29: A Leader's Flight: The Way of the Eagle 73
Day 30: The Sycamore Tree 75
Day 31: The Joshua Tree 77

Closing Reflection: Moving Forward 79

Closing Prayer 81

About the Book.. 83

About the Author 84

Dedication

To Bubba

Acknowledgements

To My Beloved Daddy Carl — *thank you for being my first and finest example of strength wrapped in gentleness. You taught me that true leadership begins with humility and that wisdom often speaks softly but carries the weight of heaven. Your quiet faith, steady hands, and unwavering belief in me have been the roots beneath every dream I've dared to grow.*

This book stands as one of those dreams — and it carries your imprint on every page.

To Minister Phillip Mazza — *thank you for urging me to seek God's guidance for the burden He placed on my heart. Your counsel reminded me that every calling begins in prayer, and that clarity is born from communion with the One who gives the vision.*

Foreword

"When the righteous thrive, the people rejoice; when the wicked rule, the people groan." — Proverbs 29:2 (NIV)

Leadership is holy work. It is more than strategy, charisma, or position—it is a sacred trust. Every generation faces its own leadership crisis, but the heart of the matter remains unchanged: leaders are called to serve in the Spirit of God.

As I look around today, the state of leadership grieves me. I live and work in the Washington, D.C. area, surrounded by people of great talent and commitment—yet I've watched friends and colleagues be forced into early retirement or lose their jobs with little regard for kindness, empathy, or love. The workplace, and in many ways our society, has become an arena of survival rather than service. In the words of one of America's forefathers, democracy can only endure if its citizens elect *virtuous leaders*. What I see today tells me that we are in danger of losing that virtue.

When I took my concerns to one of the ministers at my church, he listened carefully and said something that stopped me: "The Lord has put a burden on your heart to do something." I realized he was right. This book—and the others that will follow in this *Leadership for Such a Time as This* series—were born from that burden.

These reflections are not written from a place of criticism but of compassion. They are my attempt to help leaders reconnect their spiritual lives with their leadership practice—to bridge the gap between faith and function, calling and character. Each page offers an opportunity to pause, to breathe, and to listen for the still, small voice of God in the midst of leadership's noise and demands.

My hope is that these meditations bring healing to weary leaders, courage to those facing hard choices, and clarity to those who want to lead not by might or power, but by His Spirit.

May every reader who turns these pages learn or rediscover the joy of virtuous leadership—and may the Spirit of the Lord rest upon you: the Spirit of wisdom and understanding, the Spirit of counsel and might, the Spirit of knowledge and the fear of the Lord.

— *Dr. Linda Cureton*
Mitchellville, Maryland

Introduction:
Leading in the Spirit

Leadership is not simply a role to be performed; it is a sacred trust to be stewarded. Whether we lead in the church, the boardroom, the classroom, or the community, God calls us to lead in alignment with His Spirit. This book, *Leading in the Spirit: Foundations of Leadership*, is written for those who desire to honor that call.

Each reflection in these pages invites you to pause from the pace of leadership and listen for the quiet whisper of God's wisdom. These are not quick reads or leadership tips, but spiritual meditations—rooted in Scripture, drawn from experience, and meant to deepen your connection between faith and function.

You will find lessons from biblical leaders who led with courage and conviction, and from contemporary experiences that reveal how faith and leadership intersect in real life. Each devotional follows a rhythm: **Scripture**, **story**, **application**, and **reflection**. This structure is intentional—it allows both your head and your heart to engage, inviting transformation rather than mere information.

You may choose to read one devotional each day, allowing the message to linger in prayer throughout the day, or spend time each week with a single reflection, letting it shape your leadership practice over time. However you approach it, I encourage you to bring an open heart, a listening spirit, and a willingness to let God speak to your leadership journey.

These pages were born from a burden the Lord placed on my heart—a deep concern for the state of leadership in our time. In a culture that often prizes charisma over character and ambition over virtue, I believe God is calling us back to Spirit-led leadership—leadership marked by integrity, empathy, and grace. These reflections have been healing for me, and I pray they will bring the same renewal to you.

May this book remind you that you were called to lead, not because of your strength, but because of your surrender. True leadership flows from the presence of God, and when you lead in His Spirit, your influence becomes not only effective, but eternal.

As you move through these pages, remember, you are not alone on this journey. God continues to raise up leaders in every generation who are willing to listen, to serve, and to lead with virtue. This book is only the beginning. It is the first step in a greater journey toward Spirit-led leadership—a journey explored more deeply through the *Leadership for Such a Time as This* series.

About the Series

Leadership for Such a Time as This is a devotional series for those who sense that leadership is more than strategy or success—it is a sacred calling. In an age marked by division, uncertainty, and moral fatigue, God is still raising up leaders who are willing to be guided by His Spirit, grounded in virtue, and committed to serving with integrity.

Each book in this series invites leaders to pause, reflect, and rediscover the spiritual foundations of their leadership. Through Scriptures, stories, and prayerful meditations, these devotionals help leaders cultivate wisdom, humility, and courage—qualities that are not only timeless, but urgently needed in today's world.

Together, these volumes form a spiritual companion for leaders who long to lead with purpose and power—*not by might, nor by power, but by His Spirit.*

A Personal Word

These devotionals stem from decades of leadership experience in both the public and private sectors, including executive roles in the federal government and private enterprises. They are born from the intersection of real-world leadership challenges and timeless biblical truth. Every story shared is a lived experience; every principle offered has been tested in the crucible of actual leadership responsibility.

Leadership is both a privilege and a responsibility. My prayer is that these reflections will encourage you in the privilege and sustain you in the burden as you discover what it means to truly lead in the Spirit.

Dr. Linda Cureton

Week 1:

Foundation and Calling

"Before I formed you in the womb I knew you, before you were born I set you apart; I appointed you as a prophet to the nations." —Jeremiah 1:5 (NIV)

Leadership begins with calling. This first week establishes the foundation for everything that follows with the understanding that leadership is not about personal ambition but divine assignment; not about human qualification but spiritual formation.

Dr. Linda Cureton

Day 1:

A Leader's Desert Experience

"Now Moses was tending the flock of Jethro his father-in-law, the priest of Midian, and he led the flock to the far side of the wilderness and came to Horeb, the mountain of God. There the angel of the Lord appeared to him in flames of fire from within a bush. Moses saw that though the bush was on fire it did not burn up." —Exodus 3:1–2 (NIV)

Leadership often feels like a journey through the desert—isolating, barren, and filled with trials that test endurance and faith. Moses, one of the greatest leaders in history, spent forty years in the wilderness before his divine calling. His desert experience was not a punishment, but a preparation. The solitude refined him, stripping away distractions and positioning him to hear from God. When he least expected it, in the midst of isolation, he encountered the burning bush—an undeniable call to leadership.

Like Moses, many leaders find themselves in a "desert season"—a place of challenges, unexpected hardships, or career transitions. It may feel lonely, but it is often where the most profound transformation occurs. The desert teaches reliance on God, resilience in the face of adversity, and the ability to lead with wisdom.

Moses' years in Midian were not wasted—they were years of preparation. Those quiet, humbling years in the desert shaped his character and strengthened his resolve for the far greater leadership challenge that awaited him. In the wilderness, where distractions fade and pride is stripped away, leaders are formed in silence and solitude. It was there that Moses encountered God in the burning bush, a reminder that divine revelation often comes when we are still enough to listen (Psalm 46:10).

Just as the Hebrews endured forty years of wandering before reaching the Promised Land, true leadership requires perseverance through hardship and uncertainty. The wilderness teaches dependence, faith, and endurance. When Moses doubted his ability to lead, God's promise—"I will be with you"—became his anchor. That same assurance remains for every leader today: God's presence is the sustaining power that turns fear into faith and preparation into promotion.

Leadership Application

Desert seasons are not detours from your leadership calling—they are preparation for it. Use this time to develop spiritual disciplines, deepen your character, and learn to hear God's voice above the noise of external pressures.

Reflection

- What "desert experience" has shaped your leadership?
- How can you shift your perspective to see it as preparation rather than punishment?

Day 2:

Embracing Your Divine Calling

"Before I formed you in the womb I knew you, before you were born I set you apart; I appointed you as a prophet to the nations." —Jeremiah 1:5 (NIV)

Leadership is more than a position—it is a calling. Understanding and embracing this divine calling is essential for those entrusted with leading others. God calls individuals to step into their purpose with courage and faith, recognizing that our leadership is part of His greater plan. This empowers us to serve with conviction and integrity.

When God called Jeremiah, He didn't choose him because of his experience or eloquence. In fact, Jeremiah protested, saying he was too young and didn't know how to speak. But God's response was clear: *"Do not say, 'I am too young.' You must go to everyone I send you to and say whatever I command you"* (Jeremiah 1:7 NIV). God's calling isn't based on our perceived qualifications—it's based on His sovereign choice and our willingness to obey.

This same principle applies to leadership today. You may feel unprepared, unqualified, or uncertain about your ability to lead effectively, but if God has placed you in a position of influence, it's not an accident. He knew you before you were born, and He has equipped you with everything you need to fulfill His purposes through your leadership.

Every leader is called for a purpose, uniquely designed by God. Recognizing that divine assignment is the foundation of authentic leadership. When leaders understand and embrace their specific mission, they lead with clarity, confidence, and humility—no longer striving to imitate others, but rather fulfilling the work that God alone has entrusted to them.

Adversity is an unavoidable companion on the journey of leadership. Yet faith transforms trials into testimonies. When the path forward is uncertain, trusting God's direction enables leaders to walk boldly, knowing that every obstacle can serve as preparation for greater purpose. The leader who walks by faith learns that victory often begins in surrender.

True leadership is never about elevating oneself—it's about empowering others. Great leaders create spaces where others can grow, contribute, and thrive. They recognize the gifts within their teams and cultivate them, helping others discover their own God-given potential. In doing so, they multiply impact and legacy.

Finally, leadership is not a destination but a continual process of growth. Wise leaders remain teachable, seeking knowledge, counsel, and spiritual insight. By staying attuned to God's guidance, they remain adaptable, grounded, and effective in every season of change.

Leadership Application

Take time to reflect on how God has uniquely equipped you for your current leadership role. What experiences, skills, and perspectives has He given you that others in your position might not have? Lead from that place of divine design.

Reflection

- How does your leadership align with God's calling for your life?
- What steps can you take to lead with greater faith, courage, and intentionality?

Day 3:

Masterpiece: Destined for Greatness

"For we are God's masterpiece. He has created us anew in Christ Jesus, so we can do the good things he planned for us long ago."—Ephesians 2:10 (NLT)

You are not a mistake. You are not an accident. You are not the sum of your flaws or failures. You are God's workmanship—His *poema*, His masterpiece. Before time began, God imagined you, designed you, and wrote a destiny over your life that is uniquely yours. As a leader, this truth is your bedrock. Your leadership is not just a role—it is a calling sculpted by divine hands.

Being fearfully and wonderfully made (Psalm 139:14) means you carry the fingerprints of your Creator in every fiber of your being. Your voice, your insight, your presence—all of it has a place in God's grand narrative. The divine Artist did not leave you incomplete or ill-equipped. He fashioned you with purpose, skill, and intention.

But destiny is not passive. Ephesians 2:10 says we are created for *good works*, and those works were prepared and planned before we were born. Your leadership assignment is not random—it is a sacred path laid out by God Himself. Your influence, your courage, your vision—they are all instruments God uses to execute His plans on earth through you.

Still, there will be times when you doubt your worth or feel inadequate in the face of complex decisions and mounting challenges.

In those moments, remember: Your worth is never tied to performance. It is established by the One who made you. You are leading from a place of design, not accident; from calling, not coincidence.

This is your destiny: to lead as God's masterpiece, fulfilling the good works He has already imagined you walking in.

Leadership Application

Embrace your unique design and lead with confidence in God's intention for your life. Stop comparing yourself to other leaders and start operating from your divine blueprint.

Reflection

- What would shift in your leadership if you genuinely believed you were God's masterpiece?
- In what ways are you walking in the good works God prepared for you?
- Where do you need to reclaim the confidence that comes from your divine design?

Day 4:

Leading Through Transition

"Have I not commanded you? Be strong and courageous. Do not be afraid; do not be discouraged, for the Lord your God will be with you wherever you go." —Joshua 1:9 (NIV)

Transition in leadership is inevitable. Whether stepping into a new role, following in the footsteps of a great leader, or guiding an organization through change, the process is often marked by uncertainty and challenge. The story of Joshua, who was tasked with leading the Israelites after Moses' death, provides powerful lessons in transitional leadership. Joshua's mission was monumental—he had to fill the shoes of one of history's greatest leaders while guiding an entire nation into the Promised Land.

Much like the resilient Joshua tree in the desert, leaders navigating transition must be deeply rooted in faith, adaptable, and unwavering in their mission. The Joshua tree's branches reach toward the sky, symbolizing hope and perseverance. Similarly, leaders must stretch beyond their comfort zones, trusting that God's presence will sustain them in times of uncertainty.

Joshua was not just a leader—he was a prepared leader. He had spent years serving under Moses, learning, observing, and strengthening his faith. When the time came for him to step up, he did so with confidence in God's promise. He embraced the transition with faith, knowing that God was with him every step of the way.

Change can be daunting, but God calls us to lean on His strength. When transitions arise, His command to be strong and courageous is both a comfort and a charge. Trusting in His guidance allows us to navigate new seasons with confidence, knowing that He equips us for every step of the journey.

Joshua's leadership was effective because he had prepared. Years spent learning from Moses shaped his wisdom and character. Likewise, leaders today must embrace growth—seeking mentorship, gaining new knowledge, and allowing God to refine them for greater responsibility. Preparation is not wasted time; it is sacred training for what's next.

Transitional leadership requires both continuity and vision. Joshua never wavered from the mission God had set before him. He led with clarity, inspiring the people by keeping their eyes on the promise rather than the obstacles.

Finally, no leader stands alone. Just as Moses supported Joshua, wise leaders surround themselves with trusted counsel and godly mentors. Strength multiplies in community, and humility invites the kind of support that sustains leadership through every transition.

Leadership Application

Approach transitions as opportunities for growth rather than obstacles to overcome. Use transitional seasons to clarify your vision and strengthen your dependence on God.

Reflection

- What transition are you facing in your leadership journey?
- How can you prepare yourself spiritually and practically to embrace change with courage?

Day 5:

A Mentor

"And what you have heard from me in the presence of many witnesses entrust to faithful men who will be able to teach others also." —2 Timothy 2:2 (ESV)

Mentor—a name first found in Homer's *Odyssey*—was the trusted friend left to guide young Telemachus while Odysseus was away. Yet there's a fascinating layer to the story: The goddess Athena often appeared in the shape of Mentor, offering divine counsel and protection.

It wasn't merely human wisdom that led Telemachus forward; it was divine inspiration flowing through a human relationship. Telemachus found courage, purpose, and vision because someone—divinely empowered—walked beside him.

I've felt the ache of needing a mentor. Throughout my professional journey, I yearned for someone wise to guide me, help me navigate complex paths, open doors, and offer a valuable perspectives. Yet despite all my searching, I often felt alone in the climb.

Then one day, a chance encounter changed my life. Someone said to me, "The best way to find a mentor is to be a mentor."

Yes, of course. The best way to receive is to give. What a wonderful leadership paradox.

Paul echoes this same principle in his letter to Timothy: *"And what you have heard from me…entrust to faithful men who will be able to teach others also"* (2 Timothy 2:2). Divine wisdom isn't meant to stop with us. We're called to pass it on, creating an unbroken chain of leaders, teachers, and mentors who carry forward God's truth.

Leadership, like mentorship, is often where human relationships become vessels for divine inspiration. Sometimes, like Athena through Mentor, God chooses to speak through us—quietly, powerfully—guiding others toward their purpose.

In becoming the mentor we once searched for, we discover that God meets our own needs in ways we never expected. We not only help others see farther; we ourselves gain clarity, courage, and joy.

Leadership Application

Stop waiting for the perfect mentor to appear and start mentoring others. In giving away what you've learned, you'll often find the guidance you've been seeking.

Reflection

- What does waiting for a mentor look like in your current season of leadership?
- How might God be inviting you to be the mentor instead?
- Who could you guide, encourage, or invest in today—passing on the wisdom and faith that others once shared with you?

Day 6:

Called Without Talent?

"'Oh, my Lord, I am not eloquent…but I am slow of speech and of tongue.' Then the Lord said to him, 'Who has made man's mouth? … Now therefore go, and I will be with your mouth and teach you what you shall speak.'" —Exodus 4:10–12 (ESV)

I was at the piano, accompanying a woman who felt called to sing. She had respiratory problems—half a lung down—and still believed God wanted her to record an album. That alone was moving. But she had no vocal talent. And I'm not saying that critically—just truthfully.

We spent a whole hour in the studio, trying to get her to come in on beat four. She couldn't hear it. She couldn't find it. And I sat there, wondering: *Does God call us to do things in areas where we have no talent? Is my judgment off? Am I just being too judgmental?*

Moses had a similar dilemma. He didn't feel eloquent enough for what God was calling him to do. But God didn't send Moses because of his talent—He sent him with His presence. That's the kind of God we serve. He calls the insecure, the unqualified, the tone-deaf, even. Not always for outcomes. Sometimes, for obedience.

And maybe that woman wasn't called to produce a chart-topping record. Maybe her calling was to show up anyway. To trust God with the breath she had. To worship with the voice she was given, not the one she wished for.

And maybe I wasn't called to be her critic. Maybe I was called to be her accompanist—in music and in mercy.

Leadership Application

Don't dismiss your calling or someone else's because it doesn't align with conventional measures of talent or qualification. God often chooses the unlikely to accomplish His purposes.

Reflection

- Have you ever dismissed someone's calling because they didn't look the part? Why?
- Have you ever questioned your own judgment because you didn't feel qualified? How did that change your feelings?
- What would change if you led with obedience instead of outcomes?

Day 7:

Pursue

"And David enquired at the Lord, saying, Shall I pursue after this troop? Shall I overtake them? And he answered him, Pursue: for thou shalt surely overtake them, and without fail recover all." —1 Samuel 30:8 (KJV)

Leadership is often glamorized as strategic foresight, decisive action, and unshakeable confidence. But in 1 Samuel 30, we find King David in one of his lowest leadership moments. His home base, Ziklag, has been raided and burned. Families, including his own, have been taken captive. His men, devastated and furious, turn their grief toward him. They speak of stoning their leader.

What does David do? He doesn't retreat into his title, his experience, or even his past victories. He reaches for the ephod—a sacred garment used to inquire of God—and he asks a simple, desperate question: "Shall I pursue?"

God's answer is as sharp as it is short: Pursue.

That one word carried the full weight of heaven's authority. It wasn't a suggestion; it was a divine command, a holy green light, and a guarantee. Pursue. Overtake. Recover all. No strategy session. No poll. Just a leader aligned with the heart of God.

As we rise in influence and accumulate successes, there's a danger that settles in—the illusion that we always know what to do. Our résumés get longer, and our prayers get shorter. We start to lean on intellect, instincts, and checklists instead of the wisdom that only comes from time in God's presence.

David could have acted out of impulse or pride. Instead, he modeled a leadership move we must model. He asked the Lord a question. He stopped. He humbled himself. He sought guidance. He listened.

Leadership is not just about moving—it's about moving with God. And sometimes, all you need is one word to get started again.

Now find your ephod.

Leadership Application

Before making major leadership decisions, create space to seek the Lord's guidance. Develop practices that help you discern God's direction rather than relying solely on human wisdom.

Reflection

- When was the last time you paused to petition the Lord before making a leadership decision?
- What are those areas in your leadership where you've leaned more on experience than divine guidance?
- What is your "ephod"—the intentional practice or space that reconnects you to God's direction?
- If God gave you one word today, how would use courage and clarity to follow it?

Week 2:

Character and Integrity

"If anyone would be first, he must be last of all and servant of all." —Mark 9:35 (ESV)

Character is the foundation upon which all effective leadership rests. This week focuses on the internal qualities that distinguish leaders who leave lasting, positive impact from those who merely occupy positions of authority.

Dr. Linda Cureton

Day 8:

Boots Before Horses

"If anyone would be first, he must be last of all and servant of all." —Mark 9:35 (ESV)

Leadership is not a platform for privilege—it is a mantle of service. I once had a boss—let's call her Marjorie—who had risen through the ranks and earned a measure of power and prestige. But over time, she began to lose touch with those who actually made the work happen.

The final straw came when the director mentioned that his secretary needed a color printer to do her job. In response, Marjorie bought two color laser printers—one for the director and one for herself. The secretary, who had the actual need, received nothing.

While Marjorie was on vacation, the director blew a gasket. Furious and fed up, he made the decision to reassign her. She called me before returning to work, sensing something was off, and asked what she should do.

I told her, "Don't come back to work. You see, the director is the kind of leader who would rather have new boots for his men than a new horse for himself."

She didn't understand what I meant.

Here's what I meant: Some leaders get caught up in the trappings of position—titles, offices, perks—and forget the people who make everything work. The frontline workers. The quiet contributors. Those who don't receive awards or invitations to meetings, but who keep the organization alive.

If they don't have what they need, if they're overlooked, ignored, or under-resourced, your leadership has failed, regardless of how impressive your title or how new your printer is.

There's a saying I love, which came from Simon Sinek, the British-American author and motivational speaker: Leaders eat last. If you're at a potluck lunch, be at the back of the line. Don't assign yourself the luxuries of leadership while the people you lead are struggling to do their jobs.

Leadership Application

True leadership is measured not by what you accumulate, but by what you give. The best leaders sacrifice personal gain to empower those they lead.

Reflections

- Are you leading from the front in title but from the back in service? Why?
- What can you give up so your team can thrive?

Day 9:

Guarding Against Greed

"Then he said to them, 'Watch out! Be on your guard against all kinds of greed; life does not consist in an abundance of possessions." —Luke 12:15 (NIV)

In this passage, Jesus gives a strong warning: "Be on your guard." He doesn't say be careful only when times are good or when wealth seems within reach. He says beware of every kind of greed—the subtle ways it can creep in when we compare ourselves to others, when we begin to measure success by what we have instead of who we are in Him.

Greed isn't about having resources. It's about when resources have us—when wanting more overshadows gratitude, integrity, and trust in God's provision. It shows up when we start believing that if we could get that one more thing, we'd finally be satisfied.

But life, as Jesus reminds us, doesn't consist of titles, bank accounts, or possessions. It consists of a heart aligned with God, one that seeks His kingdom above all else.

As leaders, ambition itself isn't sinful. God calls us to steward our gifts, lead with excellence, and multiply what He entrusts to us. But when ambition crosses into self-centered striving—when it becomes about status or accumulation rather than service and purpose—it turns into the very thing Jesus warns us about.

The antidote to greed isn't poverty. It's contentment. It's leading with open hands, ready to use what God provides for His purposes, not just our own agendas.

Leadership Application

Regularly examine your motivations. Are you pursuing advancement to serve others better or to accumulate more for yourself? Let contentment, not comparison, guide your leadership decisions.

Reflection

Where do you need to trade the restless pursuit of "more" for the peace of trusting God's provision today?

Day 10:

The Power of Words

"The tongue has the power of life and death, and those who love it will eat its fruit." —Proverbs 18:21 (NIV)

Words are powerful tools that can build up or tear down, encourage or discourage, heal or hurt. A simple change in phrasing can transform someone's entire experience, highlighting the profound impact our words can have on others.

In the Bible, James 3:5–6 compares the tongue to a small spark that can set a great forest on fire, emphasizing the significant influence our words carry. As leaders and followers of Christ, we are called to use our words wisely, speaking life, hope, and truth into the lives of those around us.

Words hold tremendous power—they can build up or break down, heal or harm. Scripture reminds us that leaders are especially accountable for how they speak. Ephesians 4:29 urges us to use words that uplift and strengthen, offering encouragement that meets others where they are. A leader's language should be a source of hope, clarity, and affirmation, shaping environments where people feel valued and inspired to grow.

Colossians 4:6 calls us to speak with grace and compassion, letting our words be "seasoned with salt." This means leading conversations with kindness and empathy, aware that our tone and intent can leave lasting imprints. A gracious word, delivered with understanding, can restore trust, soothe tension, and reflect the heart of Christ in moments of challenge.

Wisdom also teaches us to be mindful of timing. Proverbs 15:23 reminds us that "a timely word is a joy." Knowing when to speak—and when to stay silent—is a mark of mature leadership. A well-placed word can guide a team, comfort a heart, or diffuse a conflict, while hasty speech can do lasting damage.

Finally, James 1:19 reminds us to be "quick to listen, slow to speak, and slow to become angry." Reflection before response cultivates discernment and peace. In pausing to listen and consider, leaders not only choose better words but also model humility and self-control—virtues that make their influence both trusted and transformative.

Leadership Application

Before speaking in leadership situations, pause and consider:

- Will these words build up or tear down?
- Will they bring clarity or confusion?
- Will they encourage or discourage?

Reflection

- Consider a time when someone's words had a profound impact on you—either positively or negatively.
- How can you be more intentional with your words to ensure they bring life and encouragement to others?

Day 11:

Skeletons and the Spirit

"And I will put my Spirit within you, and you shall live, and I will place you in your own land. Then you shall know that I am the Lord; I have spoken, and I will do it, declares the Lord."
—Ezekiel 37:14 (ESV)

We all have skeletons. Regrets, failures, or painful moments we've locked away, buried deep in the closets of our memory. We lead, we preach, and we pretend while hoping no one opens that door. The shame, the brokenness, the secrets. We fear they will disqualify us. So, we keep them hidden.

But God doesn't deal in concealment. He deals in resurrection.

In Ezekiel 37, God leads the prophet to a valley filled with dry bones—not hidden in a closet but scattered in plain view. They represent death, despair, and the fractured identity of a people. Yet God tells Ezekiel to speak to them. As he obeys, the bones rattle, reconnect, grow flesh, and finally receive breath. What was once dead becomes a living army.

What if your skeletons aren't meant to stay hidden? What if they are dry bones waiting for God's breath? God doesn't expose to humiliate—He reveals to heal. He transforms what we buried in shame into a testimony of grace. But we must open the closet. We must speak the truth. And we must allow the Spirit to enter what we've long tried to keep sealed.

For leaders, this is essential. The world doesn't need perfect images—it needs restored people. When God breathes into your dead places, your leadership gains a depth, humility, and power that no polished persona can match.

Don't let the enemy keep your past in hiding. Let God redeem it. Let Him breathe on it. Then, stand and lead—not as one haunted, but as one raised.

Leadership Application

Consider how your past failures and struggles when surrendered to God can become sources of wisdom and empathy that strengthen rather than weaken your leadership.

Reflection

- What have you buried that God wants to restore?
- What are some ways that you can let Him breathe on your dry bones?

Day 12:

When God Is Listening

"If I had cherished iniquity in my heart, the Lord would not have listened. But truly God has listened; He has attended to the voice of my prayer." —Psalm 66:18–19 (ESV)

A leader I was mentoring once asked, "What's the best way to show gratitude to my organization?" He was struggling—not with saying thank you, but with how to do it in a way that felt honest and effective. Morale was low, and his team sensed something was off. They weren't feeling appreciated, no matter what he said or did.

I told him: The best way to show gratitude is to *actually be* grateful.

Psalm 66 challenges us to go beyond performance and into the heart. Verse 18 reminds us that what we harbor inside matters. Leadership is not just about public actions, but also about private alignment. As the saying goes, character is what you do when no one is watching—but maybe even more important is this question: What do you think or harbor in your heart when God is listening?

Because—according to verse 19—He is listening.

Leadership requires more than the right words or well-timed gestures. It requires the correct alignment. Before my mentee could decide how to show gratitude, he had to reflect on the sincere reason he was grateful. Once he got his heart right—aligned his feelings, intentions, and values—the "how" became clear. Gratitude flowed more naturally, and the team felt it.

Leadership Application

Authentic leadership starts in the heart. Actions without alignment ring hollow. If you want to lead with gratitude, start by cultivating it within. Get your heart right first—because God is listening, and so are your people.

Reflection

- What unspoken thoughts or motives are living in your heart?
- Are they aligned with the values you want your leadership to reflect?

Day 13:

Strength in Stillness

"Come to me, all who labor and are heavy laden, and I will give you rest." —Matthew 11:28 (ESV)

I didn't always think rest was necessary. As a systems programmer—a programmer's programmer—rest was something for the weak and uncaffeinated. My world was uptime and performance. When something went awry, it wasn't just an inconvenience; it impacted thousands of users. I once came into the office, greeted my boss with a cheerful "Good morning," and was met with a curt "Go to the computer room."

What I found was a dreadful silence. The white noise from the powerful hum of the mainframe was gone. I came to work on a Monday and didn't leave (nor eat nor sleep) until Wednesday. No food. No sleep. A pot of coffee—not a cup—was my constant companion. In those days, eating and sleeping felt like luxuries or indulgences I couldn't afford. I was proud of my stamina and self-sufficiency. But in hindsight, I realize that was not a strength. It was pride.

God opposes the proud but gives grace to the humble. And even God—Creator of the cosmos—rested. If the Lord of the Universe saw fit to pause, what makes us believe we're above rest? As leaders, we carry heavy burdens, make weighty decisions, and often feel the pressure to perform at all costs. But Jesus extends a different invitation: *"Come to me...and I will give you rest."*

Rest isn't weakness. It is wisdom. It takes courage to admit we are weary. It takes strength to ask for help. To rest is to trust that the world will keep spinning even when we stop. It is an act of humility and faith.

Let us redefine what strength looks like in leadership—not in endless striving but in surrender. Not in burnout, but in balance. Because God's design for us includes rest—sacred, restoring, soul-deep rest.

Leadership Application

Build rhythms of rest into your leadership practice. Model healthy boundaries for your team by demonstrating that rest is not a sign of laziness, but rather a sign of wisdom.

Reflection

- Where in your leadership are you pushing beyond your limits without rest?
- What beliefs are keeping you from accepting Christ's invitation to rest?
- How can embracing sacred rest actually make you a stronger and wiser leader?

Day 14:

The Road Less Traveled

"Enter by the narrow gate. For the gate is wide and the way is easy that leads to destruction, and those who enter by it are many. For the gate is narrow and the way is hard that leads to life, and those who find it are few." —Matthew 7:13–14 (ESV)

Leadership often requires choices that defy convention and popularity. In Matthew's gospel, Jesus speaks of two gates: one wide and easy, the other narrow and hard. The wide gate is popular—it accommodates the crowd. But the narrow gate, which leads to life, is chosen by few. This isn't just about salvation; it reflects the deeper principle that paths of righteousness, purpose, and authentic leadership are rarely overcrowded.

I recall selecting my doctoral dissertation topic: chaos and complexity. Everyone else seemed to gravitate toward safer, more conventional topics. But I went solo, not only because I preferred working alone, but because I sensed this was my unique lane. I didn't want to walk the well-trodden path; I wanted to forge one of my own.

In leadership, the road less traveled is often the path of integrity over popularity, of vision over comfort, of principle over expediency. It's rarely easy and often misunderstood. But those willing to walk it find a depth of growth and clarity that the broad road could never offer.

Leadership Application

The narrow path is not just about doing what others won't—it's about doing what few can. It requires courage to reject the crowd's approval and follow a divine compass. As a leader, ask yourself not "What's trending?" but "What's true?" Your purpose may not come with a crowd, but it will come with power, clarity, and peace.

Reflection

- Where in your leadership journey have you faced a choice between the narrow and wide path?
- What helped you choose the road less traveled—and what have you learned from that decision?

Week 3:

Spiritual Discernment

"But when he, the Spirit of truth, comes, he will guide you into all the truth. He will not speak on his own; he will speak only what he hears, and he will tell you what is yet to come." — John 16:13 (NIV)

Leadership requires more than strategic thinking—it demands spiritual discernment. This week focuses on cultivating the ability to hear God's voice, recognize His guidance, and respond with obedience in the complex decisions that define effective leadership.

Day 15:

Burning Bush Moments

"When the Lord saw that he turned aside to see, God called to him out of the bush, 'Moses, Moses!' And he said, 'Here I am.'" —Exodus 3:4 (ESV)

As leaders, we often seek God in our strategic planning, pray before major decisions, and look for signs when the path seems uncertain. But how often do we pause long enough to actually notice when God answers?

I remember a moment clearly—one of triumph and transition. I had just completed a large, high-visibility project. It was successful, impactful, and praised. Naturally, I thought, *Now's the perfect time to move on. This win will open doors.* I was ready to leverage the moment for the next step.

Then came the burning bush.

It was early morning. My admin, a righteous woman of God, came in earlier than usual, looking tired. She shut the door behind her and said, "Dear, I pray for you all the time. And the Lord put something on my heart last night, and I barely slept."

Now, church folk say that often—but when she said it, I knew to pay attention.

She continued, "The Lord told me you shouldn't leave just yet. You need to see this implementation through."

I cried. Not because I didn't trust her words—but because I already knew they were true. God had spoken through her. Not in thunder or fire—but in a quiet office, through a faithful messenger.

Burning-bush moments aren't always miraculous spectacles. Sometimes, they show up as weary voices, unexpected conversations, or deep convictions that you can't shake. The question is, are we paying attention?

Leadership Application

God still speaks to leaders. Not always with drama—but always with purpose. Your job is not just to pray for answers, but to stay sensitive enough to recognize when the answer appears. And once you hear it, the faithful response is obedience—even when it disrupts your plans.

Reflection

- Have you experienced a burning-bush moment in your leadership journey?
- Did you notice it? And more importantly—did you listen?

Day 16:

Faith and Works: Vision with Action

"So also faith by itself, if it does not have works, is dead."
—James 2:17 (ESV)

There's a management principle that says, "A vision without a plan is hallucination." It's clever—and it's true. We often assume that having faith is enough, but Scripture reminds us otherwise. Faith without action is meaningless. But let's not forget the converse: Actions without faith are lifeless. Both are essential. One without the other is empty.

I once led an agency-wide help-desk implementation—a massive project that had the potential to transform our organization. On paper, it had all the right pieces: the plan, the people, the process. But it failed. Not because the team was unqualified, but because I never believed in them. Deep down, I didn't trust that they could pull it off, and that lack of faith shaped every decision I made.

The turnaround didn't come from a new tool or a better process—it came from humility. I sat down with every team member, one-on-one. I listened, I learned, and I realized, the failure wasn't theirs. It was mine. I hadn't led with faith. I had work plans, charts, and metrics—but I had starved the team of belief, trust, and vision.

Leadership is more than strategy. It is a belief in people. It is hope in outcomes yet unseen. God reveals this balance through the union of faith and works. We must dream boldly but also act intentionally. We must work with excellence but also believe fervently. One without the other will falter.

Let your leadership be rooted in this divine symphony, paired with action, and that action infused with belief.

Leadership Application

Examine your current leadership approach. Are you relying too heavily on strategy without faith in your people, or are you relying too heavily on faith without concrete action? Seek the balance that honors both divine vision and practical execution.

Reflection

- Are you leaning too heavily on plans without belief—or on belief without a concrete plan?
- What project or team needs more of your faith right now?
- What step can you take today to align your vision with meaningful action?

Day 17:

Becoming the Answer to Prayers

"Therefore I tell you, whatever you ask in prayer, believe that you have received it, and it will be yours." —Mark 11:24 (ESV)

As we grow in leading in the Spirit, we discover the power of petitioning God—not timidly but believing. Jesus taught His disciples to pray with expectation: to ask boldly, to seek persistently, and to trust the Father's response. Yet prayer carries a mystery: sometimes we are not the ones to receive the answer, but we are the ones sent to be it.

I learned this when I found myself in an urgent legal predicament late one night. I needed to file a case immediately, but waking our corporate counsel at 1:00 a.m. didn't seem like an option. I prayed, my head said "no," and I nearly stopped. Yet something kept drawing me back to "yes." Armed with divine concurrence, critical thinking, and ChatGPT, I pressed forward—and succeeded. My legal case prevailed. I moved on, thinking the matter was closed. Days later, I shared this story with a woman I had just met. To my surprise, she gasped, nearly in tears. She told me she had prayed and even dreamed that she would meet someone who could show her how to file her case using ChatGPT. My midnight struggle was her answered prayer.

I experienced this phenomenon again when stepping into a new leadership role in an organization marked by low morale and stagnation. An informal leader—benched by my predecessor—held the team's loyalty, leaving progress stalled because the team lost its leader. I reached out to him, hoping to establish a connection. His first words were blunt and almost accusatory: "Why are you here?" I offered polished, predictable answers. He pressed again. Finally, I admitted, "I don't know." He looked at me and said, "I do … Every week, we prayed at lunch that God would send a CIO to lead us out of this dark place. Then you came." In that moment, I realized I was standing in the middle of their answered prayer. His heart shifted, and he pledged, "Whatever help you need, I am here for you."

Scripture holds similar stories. Joseph told his brothers, *"God sent me before you to preserve life"* (Genesis 45:5, ESV). Esther risked her life to stand before the king *"for such a time as this"* (Esther 4:14, KJV). God consistently raises leaders as tangible responses to the prayers of His people—so that His purposes advance, His people are sustained, and His glory is revealed.

Leadership Application

Discernment is maturity. Prayer is not only about what God does for you, but also about recognizing when God is working through you. Leaders must cultivate spiritual sensitivity to see when their assignment is the very provision others have pleaded for.

Reflection

- Where might God be using you right now as the answer to someone's prayer?
- How can you sharpen your discernment to recognize divine assignments hidden in ordinary encounters?
- Are you willing not only to ask but also to be sent?

Day 18:

Found in the Wilderness

"The angel of the Lord found her by a spring of water in the wilderness, the spring on the way to Shur." —Genesis 16:7 (ESV)

Hagar wasn't trying to be seen—she was trying to disappear. After suffering mistreatment, she fled into the wilderness. She was a servant, marginalized and alone, with no voice and no options. And yet, that is exactly where God found her.

I remember my own wilderness. I had just been hired into a high-level government position, right after an election, but before a political transition. I was new to this echelon of leadership and totally unprepared for what came next. With the change in administration, I was left stranded—no boss, no direction, and a lot of judgment from people who didn't even know me. Every day got harder. And I cried every day.

At my lowest point, I developed a strange ritual. I'd go to a nearby restaurant for their warm pumpernickel bread, return to the office, send everyone home early, shut my door, and cry. That was my leadership moment.

Then one day, a friend and co-worker burst into my office, slammed the door, and said, "Babes! You gotta dry those tears and lead this organization." So, I did. Things never got better, not really. But as I look back nearly twenty-five years later, I see that those wilderness moments shaped me. God didn't remove me from the wilderness, but He met me there. And in that encounter, I managed to survive. I came out of my office. I learned. I grew.

As leaders, we long for clarity and confidence. But God often does His best work in us when we feel most abandoned. The wilderness may be where we feel least effective—but it's where God finds us and makes us strong.

Leadership Application

Don't despise seasons of isolation or difficulty. These wilderness experiences often become the crucible where authentic leadership is forged and where you learn to depend on God rather than circumstances.

Reflection

- What wilderness are you facing right now?
- How might God be using it not to weaken you, but to prepare you for the journey ahead?

Day 19:

Wait for It—God's Appointed Time

"For still the vision awaits its appointed time; it hastens to the end—it will not lie. If it seems slow, wait for it; it will surely come; it will not delay." —Habakkuk 2:3 (ESV)

As a child, I often spent carefree summer days exploring the banks of the Potomac River near an area in Maryland once known as Marshall Hall. On one such day, my sister Loreen and I, only eight and seven years old, attempted our own impromptu fishing adventure. With no real gear in hand, we fashioned a makeshift pole from a stick and some tangled line we had found. Our bait? Pieces of hot dog buns.

We waited and waited. The fish happily stole our bait while we caught nothing. Frustrated and convinced this was going nowhere, I discarded our humble creation into the river. Just as it floated away, Loreen triumphantly returned—squid in hand, the slimy promise of real bait ready for action. Her face fell when she saw our "pole" drifting beyond reach. She had waited, she had believed, and she had come prepared. I, on the other hand, gave up too soon.

God often gives us a vision—an assignment, a dream, a calling—that doesn't unfold on our schedule. In the book of Habakkuk, the prophet is reminded that God's vision has an appointed time. It may seem delayed from our perspective, but it will come. The key is to wait for it—to trust, prepare, and persevere without discarding the tools of our faith in frustration.

Leadership Application

Whether you're building a ministry, launching a business, or stewarding a team, remember: Your role is not to force God's hand, but to remain faithful until His timing arrives. Premature action can cause us to miss out on what God is about to deliver. Don't let your impatience cause you to discard what God intends to bless you with.

Reflection

- Where in your leadership are you growing impatient?
- How can you lean into God's timing and prepare in faith for what He has promised?

Day 20:

Embracing God's Non-Linear Pathways

"For my thoughts are not your thoughts, neither are your ways my ways, declares the Lord. For as the heavens are higher than the earth, so are my ways higher than your ways and my thoughts than your thoughts." —Isaiah 55:8–9 (ESV)

In our leadership journeys, we often anticipate linear progressions—clear steps leading to predictable outcomes. However, the divine narrative frequently unfolds in unexpected ways, reminding us that we do not serve a linear God. God's plans transcend our human understanding, weaving through complexities that challenge our perceptions of order and timing.

Leaders often find themselves in seasons of waiting or redirection, wondering why progress seems delayed. Yet God's timing is never arbitrary. What feels like a detour is often divine preparation—a reordering of events so that our readiness matches His purpose. Trusting in His timing means surrendering the illusion of control and believing that the delay itself may be the very thing that shapes us for the promise ahead.

Leadership in God's kingdom also requires flexibility. His guidance does not always follow a predictable path; sometimes He leads us through unexpected terrain to reveal new strength or perspective. Like Abraham journeying to an unknown land, leaders must learn to walk by faith, adjusting plans with open hands and a willing heart.

The ability to pivot, while staying anchored in purpose, is a mark of spiritual maturity.

When uncertainty clouds the path, wise leaders seek deeper understanding rather than quick answers. Through prayer and reflection, our vision aligns with God's—broad, eternal, and redemptive. In that quiet communion, He refines our motives and clarifies the next step.

Finally, patience is not passivity; it is active trust. Every stage of the journey—whether stillness or movement—serves a role in forming the leader God intends us to become. When we wait with faith, we discover that His plan is unfolding not just around us, but within us.

Leadership Application

Instead of forcing your preferred timeline or path, develop the spiritual maturity to discern when God is redirecting your steps. His detours often become the very paths that prepare you for greater impact.

Reflection

Consider areas in your leadership where you've encountered unexpected turns. How can you deepen your trust in God's non-linear pathways and remain steadfast in your mission?

Day 21:

Nothing Is Random in Divine Order

"The lot is cast into the lap, but its every decision is from the Lord." —Proverbs 16:33 (NIV)

In leadership, it is tempting to believe that success hinges on luck or chance. Many hope that opportunities will "randomly" come their way or that the right conditions will magically align for their next breakthrough. But true leadership is not about rolling the dice—it is about faith, preparation, and taking inspired action.

John von Neumann, a brilliant mathematician, once joked that relying on arithmetic to generate randomness was "a state of sin." The truth is, even in mathematics, randomness is an illusion—patterns emerge when one understands the system behind them. The same holds for leadership. When we attribute success to randomness, we rob ourselves of the responsibility to act with purpose. Waiting for "good luck" leads to inaction, while believing in divine order compels us to move forward with faith.

My NASA team once told me that they had a success-oriented schedule for one of our projects. I eventually learned that this statement was cultural code for saying they had no idea when they would finish, but they would cross their fingers and hope to get lucky. Well, luck is not a reliable management skill. Furthermore, it is a leadership pastime of the incompetent.

Scripture affirms that nothing is truly random and that luck is a fallacy. Proverbs 16:33 reminds us that even when events seem like chance (or luck), God is at work behind the scenes, directing outcomes for His purpose. Leaders must trust that their actions, guided by wisdom and faith, align with a greater plan. This belief does not eliminate uncertainty, but it transforms uncertainty into opportunity—a call to act with confidence and to embrace the divine order shaping their path.

Leadership Application

Stop waiting for perfect circumstances or lucky breaks. Instead, prepare diligently, act with faith, and trust that God is orchestrating events according to His purpose. Your faithful action positions you for His divine appointments.

Reflection

Reflect on an instance in your leadership journey where what seemed like coincidence turned out to be divine alignment. How can you step forward in faith, trusting that no detail of your path is random?

Week 4:

Leading Through Adversity

"Consider it pure joy, my brothers and sisters, whenever you face trials of many kinds, because you know that the testing of your faith produces perseverance." —James 1:2–3

Every leader faces seasons of opposition, betrayal, and overwhelming challenges. This week explores how to lead with wisdom and grace when the path becomes difficult, discovering that adversity often becomes the crucible where authentic leadership is forged.

Dr. Linda Cureton

Day 22:

Alexander the Coppersmith

"Alexander the coppersmith did me great harm; the Lord will repay him according to his deeds. Beware of him yourself, for he strongly opposed our message." —2 Timothy 4:14–15 (ESV)

Leadership is not for the faint of heart. Along the way, you will encounter individuals who actively oppose your mission, undermine your credibility, or seek to do you harm. The Apostle Paul warns Timothy about one such adversary—Alexander the Coppersmith. Though the details of Alexander's opposition are not fully recorded, his resistance was enough for Paul to caution Timothy with both a warning and a reassurance: God will handle the injustice.

As leaders, we must be vigilant against the "Alexanders" in our lives—those who challenge, resist, or attempt to derail our purpose. However, Paul does not suggest retaliation. Instead, he entrusts the matter to God. This reminds us that while opposition is inevitable, our response should be one of wisdom, prayer, and trust in God's justice.

The leadership lesson here is twofold: first, recognize opposition for what it is—sometimes a necessary confirmation that you are on the right path. Second, do not be consumed by the battle. Stay focused on the mission God has given you and let Him handle the enemies that rise against you.

Leadership Application

Document patterns of opposition and respond strategically rather than emotionally. Protect yourself with wisdom while entrusting ultimate justice to God. Don't let adversaries distract you from your divine assignment. Finally, don't take a knife to a gunfight. Meaning, don't fight spiritual warfare with carnal tools. Use the entire armor of God.

Reflection

- Who is an "Alexander" in your leadership journey?
- How can you guard yourself wisely while entrusting the outcome to God?
- Read Ephesians 6:10-18. How will you put on this armor?

Day 23:

Faithfulness in Isolation

"And God remembered Noah, and every living thing, and all the cattle that was with him in the ark: and God made a wind to pass over the earth, and the waters assuaged." —Genesis 8:1 (KJV)

Leadership can often feel like isolation. The higher you rise, the lonelier it becomes. You carry burdens others don't see, make sacrifices others don't understand, and endure seasons where affirmation and validation are scarce.

Noah knew this weight. He obeyed God's call to build an ark when there was no rain. For years, he led his family through a seemingly absurd project, misunderstood and mocked by those around him. Then came the flood—forty days of rain, followed by months adrift in a silent, endless ocean. No visible progress. No exit plan. No word from God. Just waiting.

Nevertheless, God remembered Noah.

The silence of isolation did not mean Noah was forgotten. God was working in unseen ways, preparing dry ground while Noah remained faithful in his assignment. In leadership, there will be seasons where you feel adrift—where progress seems invisible, and you wonder if your labor has been in vain.

But God's memory is perfect. He never forgets your faithfulness. His delays are not dismissals. His silence is not abandonment. He remembers every sacrifice, every prayer, every obedient step you've taken in isolation.

In business, this may mean leading a team through an uncertain market, stewarding a vision that few understand, or standing firm on convictions while others compromise. These are ark-building seasons—costly, lonely, but remembered by God.

Leadership Application

During seasons of isolation, focus on faithfulness rather than visibility. God sees what others miss and is preparing outcomes beyond your current circumstances.

Reflection

- In what ways do visible results seem distant during this season of leadership?
- How can you remain faithful while trusting that God remembers and is preparing dry ground for you?

Day 24:

Let God Fight Your Battles

"You will not have to fight this battle. Take up your positions; stand firm and see the deliverance the Lord will give you, Judah and Jerusalem. Do not be afraid; do not be discouraged. Go out to face them tomorrow, and the Lord will be with you."
—2 Chronicles 20:17 (NIV)

Leadership often feels like a constant battle—market competition, difficult personnel decisions, financial pressures, and the never-ending weight of responsibility. Every leader knows the temptation to believe that outcomes depend entirely on their strategy, their skill, and their effort.

But Jehoshaphat faced a crisis no leadership textbook could resolve. Outnumbered and outmatched, his kingdom stood on the brink of destruction. He did what effective leaders often fail to do: He sought the Lord first. The divine response was astonishing—*"You will not have to fight this battle."*

God didn't call Jehoshaphat to strategize or mobilize resources. He called him to position his people, stand still, and watch God work.

There are battles in leadership that are not ours to fight. The wisdom of leadership lies in discerning when to act and when to let go. Sometimes the most courageous leadership move is surrender—trusting that God is working in unseen ways to bring resolution, protection, and victory.

In business, this might mean releasing control over circumstances you cannot influence, such as a contract decision, unfair competition, or a complex regulatory challenge. It is not passive; it is a matter of positioning. You show up, you remain faithful, but you trust the outcome into God's hands.

When the battle belongs to the Lord, the victory will always exceed anything your human effort could achieve.

Leadership Application

Learn to distinguish between battles that require your action and those that belong to God. Position yourself faithfully and trust God to fight the battles beyond your control.

Reflection

- What current leadership battle are you fighting that God is calling you to release into his hands?
- How can you practice the discipline of positioning yourself and trusting God to fight for you?

Day 25:

Power in Vulnerability

"And he said unto me, My grace is sufficient for thee: for my strength is made perfect in weakness." —2 Corinthians 12:9 (KJV)

In the business world, strength is often equated with confidence, decisiveness, and the ability to control outcomes. Leaders are expected to project certainty, competence, and unshakable resolve. Vulnerability, by contrast, is often perceived as weakness—something to be hidden, not embraced.

But God's leadership model turns this entirely upside down.

The Apostle Paul was a brilliant leader, yet he openly acknowledged his weakness—what he referred to as his "thorn in the flesh." He pleaded with God to remove it. But God's answer was not deliverance, but dependence: *"My grace is sufficient for thee: for my strength is made perfect in weakness."*

True leadership strength is not the absence of weakness but the presence of God's grace working through it. When leaders stop pretending to have it all together, they create space for God's power to flow and for others to thrive. Vulnerability fosters trust, builds authentic relationships, and models the kind of humility that sustains organizations through crisis and complexity.

In business, this might mean admitting you don't have all the answers, seeking wise counsel, apologizing when you're wrong, or acknowledging your personal limits. Far from undermining your credibility, this kind of vulnerability deepens respect and invites collaboration.

Leadership is not about projecting invincibility—it's about embodying authenticity, where God's strength is showcased through surrendered hearts.

Leadership Application

Identify areas where you've been trying to project strength rather than acknowledge limitations. Consider how appropriate vulnerability might actually strengthen your leadership and deepen trust with your team.

Reflection

- In what areas of your leadership do you feel pressure to project strength rather than reveal honest vulnerability?
- How might God's grace meet you more fully if you surrendered those areas to Him?

Day 26:

The Judas in the Room

"Then after he had taken the morsel, Satan entered into him. Jesus said to him, 'What you are going to do, do quickly.'"
—John 13:27 (ESV)

As a leader of a three-thousand-person IT organization, I've had my fair share of Judases. People who smiled in meetings and took notes in the same strategy sessions—only to file grievances behind closed doors or undermine decisions from the shadows. And when the betrayal came, it wasn't unexpected—but it still hurt.

There were three in particular—let's call them Judas One, Two, and Three. These were women I had supported, advocated for, and positioned for success. Yet, they turned against me. They lodged complaints and framed narratives that didn't align with the truth. In other words, they lied!

At the time, I wrestled with anger, confusion, and yes, a bit of paranoia. As author John Green once said, "You're not really paranoid if everybody is against you."

But here's what time—and the Word—have taught me: Judases have a purpose.

Jesus had His Judas. And unlike the rest of us, He saw the betrayal coming and didn't flinch. He still broke bread with him. Still washed his feet. Still called him friend. Jesus knew the pain was part of the plan. Judas wasn't an accident. He was necessary.

Now, I'm not saying dealing with betrayal is easy. It's not. But it's part of the leadership path. We are not called to a Judas-free life, but to be wise, discerning, and—when the Spirit leads—merciful.

Looking back, I wonder: What would I have done differently if I had led those Judases with empathy? Could I have softened? Asked more questions? Listened more deeply? I don't know. However, I do know that empathy doesn't mean weakness—it means leading with clarity and compassion simultaneously.

Leadership Application

Betrayal is part of the leadership terrain. But don't let it harden you. Learn from it. Grow from it. And ask God not just to protect you from Judases—but to transform how you see them. Sometimes they are mirrors. Sometimes they are thorns in your side. But they are always teachers.

Reflection

- Who is *the Judas* in your leadership story?
- Can you look back and see what God was shaping in you through their betrayal?

Day 27:

Our "Jobian" Existence

"But he knows the way that I take; when he has tested me, I will come forth as gold." —Job 23:10 (NIV)

There are seasons in life where the bottom seems to fall out. For those of us who thrive on our intellect, discipline, and problem-solving skills, these moments feel especially cruel. Like Job, we enter storms we never saw coming—stripped of our confidence, blindsided by circumstances that intellect alone cannot resolve.

I recall a period in my career when I excelled due to my abilities in logic, memory, and navigating complex abstract concepts. These skills were not only beneficial, but also celebrated. But eventually, I hit a wall. It wasn't a technical problem I couldn't solve or a concept I couldn't grasp. It was people. Politics. Influence. Alliance-building. Things I wasn't equipped for.

Like Job, I suffered. I questioned myself, and I questioned God.

But suffering became a crucible. Through the pain, I learned humility, emotional intelligence, and the power of relational wisdom. What once seemed like defeat became a sacred reformation. Looking back, I see how God used what felt like professional death to bring about personal resurrection.

Viktor Frankl, who endured the unimaginable in Nazi concentration camps, once said: "Those who have a 'why' to live can bear almost any 'how.'" I believe that. When we remember our divine purpose and destiny, even the darkest seasons have meaning.

Leadership Application

Don't despise the seasons that strip away your natural strengths. These Jobian experiences often become the crucible in which deeper leadership qualities—such as empathy, resilience, and spiritual depth—are forged.

Reflection

- What Jobian trials have marked your journey?
- Are you still bitter about the pain, or can you now see the refining purpose in it?
- Leadership isn't just about strategy and success—it's also about suffering and sanctification. Let God's testing forge you into gold.

Day 28:

The Furnace of Character

"For to this you have been called, because Christ also suffered for you, leaving you an example, so that you might follow in his steps." —1 Peter 2:21 (ESV)

In the world of business leadership, there's often an unspoken assumption: If I execute with excellence, success should follow easily. We develop strategies, build teams, and drive results—all while hoping that our diligence will insulate us from failure, opposition, or hardship.

Yet, Scripture tells a different story. Peter writes that we are called to suffering—not as a punishment, but as a pathway. Even Christ, the perfect leader, endured rejection, betrayal, and ultimately, the cross. His suffering wasn't accidental; it was essential. And in following His example, we too encounter trials designed to form us, not destroy us.

Leadership in business demands resilience. Setbacks, betrayals, market disruptions, and internal conflicts test us in ways that no business school ever prepares us for. But these moments are not wasted. Like steel forged in fire, our leadership character is shaped by heat and pressure. The furnace tempers arrogance into humility, impatience into endurance, and self-interest into service.

The marketplace rewards outcomes, but God shapes leaders through the process. The pain of failed ventures, tough personnel decisions, or public criticism can feel unbearable in the moment. But in God's hands, these trials become the very tools that sharpen our discernment, deepen our empathy, and strengthen our integrity.

Leadership Application

Reframe suffering in leadership not as something to avoid, but as something that develops character. The trials you face today are forming the leader you'll become tomorrow.

Reflection

- What current leadership challenges might God be using as refining fires in your professional journey?
- How can you embrace suffering as a necessary part of becoming the leader God is calling you to be?

Week 5:

Vision and Direction

But blessed is the one who trusts in the Lord, whose confidence is in him. They will be like a tree planted by the water that sends out its roots by the stream. It does not fear when heat comes; its leaves are always green. It has no worries in a year of drought and never fails to bear fruit -- Jeremiah 17:7-8 (NIV)

A leader with vision rooted in God is like a tree planted by streams of water—steady, nourished, and unshaken by change. True direction doesn't come from ambition but from trust in the Lord. When our roots go deep in faith, we can grow upward with confidence, bearing fruit in every season and leading others with strength that endures.

Dr. Linda Cureton

Day 29:

A Leader's Flight: The Way of the Eagle

"But they who wait for the LORD shall renew their strength; they shall mount up with wings like eagles; they shall run and not be weary; they shall walk and not faint." —Isaiah 40:31 (ESV)

The eagle is one of the most potent symbols of leadership in Scripture. It embodies strength, resilience, and vision—qualities every leader must cultivate. Unlike other birds that flap tirelessly, the eagle soars, riding the wind rather than exhausting itself against it. This ability reflects a leader's need to trust in God's guidance rather than relying solely on personal effort.

Eagles have exceptional vision, enabling them to see prey from miles away. Proverbs 29:18 reminds us, *"Where there is no vision, the people perish."* Leaders must cultivate foresight, seeing beyond the immediate challenges to the opportunities ahead. An eagle's eyes remain focused, never losing sight of the goal, so, too, must leaders remain unwavering in their mission.

In Deuteronomy 32:11, God is compared to an eagle caring for its young: "Like an eagle that stirs up its nest and hovers over its young, that spreads its wings to catch them and carries them aloft." Eagles do not keep their young in the nest forever; they push them out, teaching them to fly. Great leaders develop those around them, guiding them to their own heights of achievement.

Eagles teach us profound lessons about leadership and resilience. When storms arise, eagles do not flee—they soar higher, using the wind's resistance to lift them above the turmoil. Likewise, leaders are not called to escape adversity but to rise through it. Challenges test our faith and refine our strength, becoming opportunities for growth and maturity, just as James 1:2–4 reminds us to "consider it pure joy" when trials shape our endurance.

An eagle's vision is remarkably sharp, able to focus on a target from great distances. This clarity mirrors the focus leaders must maintain amid distractions and competing demands. Proverbs 4:25 encourages us to "let your eyes look directly forward," a reminder to keep our gaze fixed on God's purpose rather than the noise around us.

Eagles also invest in the next generation, teaching their young to spread their wings and fly. Effective leaders do the same—mentoring, empowering, and preparing others to carry the mission forward. As 2 Timothy 2:2 exhorts, leadership multiplies when we entrust wisdom to faithful successors who will continue the work.

Finally, true strength is found not in striving but in surrender. Isaiah 40:31 reminds us that "those who wait on the Lord shall renew their strength." Like the eagle whose power comes from riding the wind, leaders who rely on God's Spirit find endurance that outlasts fatigue and courage that transcends circumstance.

Leadership Application

Cultivate the patience to wait for God's timing, the vision to see beyond current challenges, and the wisdom to develop others while trusting in divine strength, rather than relying solely on human effort.

Reflection

- How can you embrace the qualities of an eagle in your leadership?
- Are you soaring with God's strength, or are you flapping against the wind, exhausting yourself?

Day 30:

The Sycamore Tree

"And he ran ahead and climbed up into a sycamore tree to see him, for he was about to pass that way." —Luke 19:4 (ESV)

The sycamore tree, with its broad, heart-shaped leaves and sturdy branches, was a familiar presence in biblical landscapes. Known for its fruit and generous shade, it symbolized stability and provision. Yet beyond its physical traits, the sycamore tree offered something invaluable: elevation—a place to rise above the crowd and glimpse what lies beyond the ordinary.

For Zacchaeus, it became a place of destiny. Though he was a man of wealth and authority as a tax collector, he was small in stature and shunned by his community. The crowds blocked his view, both physically and socially. Still, something stirred within him—a longing for more, a desperate curiosity to see Jesus.

So he ran ahead and performed a single, decisive act: He climbed higher. He scaled the sycamore tree to seek a new vantage point for an unobstructed view of his salvation.

But something else happened. Not only was Zacchaeus able to see Jesus, but Jesus also saw this short little man.

Jesus looked up, locked eyes with Zacchaeus, and called him by name. In front of the very crowd that had pushed him to the margins, Zacchaeus became known, valued, and transformed. The man who climbed to see was lifted even higher by the gaze of Christ.

As leaders, we, too, must climb. We must rise above the crowd—the noise, expectations, doubts—to catch a clearer glimpse of Jesus. But here's the wonder: When we seek Him, He sees us. He knows our name, our story, our hidden battles. And His gaze has the power to transform not only how we see Him, but how we see ourselves.

Leadership calls us to courageously pursue higher ground for a new perspective. Yet even more, it calls us to remember that we are seen and known by the One who leads us.

Leadership Application

Regularly seek a higher perspective—both literally and spiritually. Find your "sycamore tree" moments where you can rise above the immediate pressures to gain clarity on God's bigger picture for your leadership.

Reflection

- What crowds are blocking your view today?
- Where might God be calling you to climb higher—not just so you can see Him, but so you can experience the profound truth that He sees you?

Day 31:

The Joshua Tree

"Have I not commanded you? Be strong and courageous. Do not be afraid; do not be discouraged, for the Lord your God will be with you wherever you go." —Joshua 1:9 (NIV)

The Joshua tree stands as a paradox of strength and surrender — its roots deeply anchored in the desert soil, its arms lifted high toward heaven. In its silhouette, we see the image of prayer, praise, and perseverance. It is as if creation itself is reaching upward in faith, declaring that even in barren places, life can flourish under God's care.

When Moses died, Joshua was called to lead a people in transition—from wilderness wandering into promise. It was a moment that required courage, vision, and faith. The tree that bears his name carries the same message: Though planted in hard places, it grows toward heaven, defying its environment with stubborn grace.

The Joshua tree also evokes another story—one that reveals the posture of leadership sustained by faith and community. As the Israelites battled the Amalekites, Moses stood on a hilltop with the staff of God raised in his hands. As long as his hands were lifted, Israel prevailed. But when fatigue overcame him, the enemy gained ground. So Aaron and Hur came beside him, holding up his arms until the sun set and victory was won (Exodus 17:8–13).

That moment is a living picture of the Joshua tree—arms outstretched in endurance, upheld by others, pointing toward the heavens in faith. It is a portrait of leadership rooted in obedience and supported by fellowship. Even the strongest leaders grow weary; even the most faithful need someone to help hold their arms steady.

Leadership Application

The Joshua tree invites us to reflect on two essential truths of leadership: We must be both deeply rooted and divinely supported. Our roots—faith, humility, integrity, prayer—keep us grounded in God's purpose. Our reach—the hands we lift, the courage we extend, the relationships that sustain us—keeps us connected to God's power.

Foundational leaders grow deep; virtuous leaders grow upward. One is anchored, the other inspired. Together, they form the full image of Spirit-led leadership—grounded in truth, reaching in grace.

So as this foundational season of draws to a close, imagine yourself as a Joshua tree in God's desert: your roots unseen but strong, your hands raised in faith, your spirit supported by others. The same God who called Joshua to cross the Jordan now calls you to rise into your next chapter—a chapter where leadership becomes not just strong, but virtuous.

Reflection

- Where do your roots draw strength—from fear or from faith?
- Who holds up your arms when leadership feels heavy?
- How is God preparing you to move from strength to virtue in this next season of growth?

Closing Reflection:
Moving Forward

As you complete *Leading in the Spirit*, you have laid a foundation that will sustain you through the leadership challenges ahead. You have explored the essential elements of called leadership: understanding your divine assignment, developing character, cultivating spiritual discernment, and leading through adversity with vision and purpose.

Leading in the Spirit is not a destination but a journey. Each day presents new opportunities to apply these principles, grow in wisdom, and serve others with integrity. As you move into the months ahead, carry with you these foundational truths:

- Your leadership is a divine calling, not a personal achievement.
- Character matters more than competence.
- Spiritual discernment guides better than human strategy.
- Adversity shapes leaders more than comfort ever could.
- God's vision for your leadership extends far beyond your own understanding.

The subsequent volumes of this series will build upon this foundation, exploring themes of vision, influence, team building, decision-making, and legacy. But everything flows from what you have established here—a heart surrendered to God's purposes and a leadership style rooted in His truth.

Continue to lead in the Spirit. The world needs leaders who serve from divine calling rather than personal ambition, who operate from spiritual wisdom rather than human cleverness alone.

Your leadership matters. Your calling is real. And God's hand is upon you as you serve Him by serving others.

Closing Prayer

Lord, You are the foundation of every faithful leader and the sustainer of every weary soul. Thank You for reminding us, through the Joshua tree, that strength begins in our roots and continues in our reach. You have called us to lead with courage, to endure with faith, and to rise with our hands lifted toward heaven.

As we bring this season of learning to a close, we consecrate our leadership to You. Root us deeper in Your Word, steady us when our arms grow tired, and surround us with those who help hold us up. May we never lead from pride or fear, but from the quiet confidence that You are with us wherever we go.

Now, as we prepare to move from foundations to virtue, from strength to grace, breathe new life into our calling. Teach us to lead with purity of heart, steadfast love, and unwavering integrity. May every decision reflect Your wisdom, every action mirror Your compassion, and every moment of leadership become an act of worship.

And now unto You who are able to keep us from falling and to present us before Your glorious presence without fault and with great joy—to the only wise God, our Savior, be glory, majesty, power, and authority, through Jesus Christ our Lord, now and forevermore. Amen.

Dr. Linda Cureton

About the Book

Leadership is not a career path—it is a calling. *Leading in the Spirit* offers thirty-one days of biblical wisdom for leaders who recognize that actual influence stems from a divine relationship, not human strategy alone.

Drawing on decades of executive experience in government and the private sector, Dr. Linda Y. Cureton explores the intersection of real-world leadership challenges and timeless biblical truth. Each devotional includes Scripture, practical leadership application, and reflection questions to shape leaders who serve with both competence and character.

From discovering your divine calling to leading through adversity with vision, this foundational volume lays the bedrock principles that sustain leaders in the face of complexity and change.

This is volume one of the *Leadership for Such a Time as This* series—an invitation to lead with courage, faith, and Spirit-filled purpose.

About the Author

Dr. Linda Cureton brings decades of executive leadership experience from both the federal government and private enterprise to the intersection of faith and leadership. Having served as Chief Information Officer for major government agencies, including NASA, and having led IT organizations with over 3,000 personnel, she understands the real-world challenges leaders face daily. Dr. Cureton is currently the Chief Executive Officer of Muse Technologies, a strategy, planning, and operations consulting firm. Her leadership journey has taken her through desert seasons, political transitions, and complex organizational transformations—experiences that have shaped her understanding of what it means to lead in the Spirit. In addition to her three degrees in mathematics, Dr. Cureton holds a Doctor of Philosophy in organizational leadership, with a focus on chaos and complexity, and is passionate about mentoring the next generation of Christian leaders.

See our contact information and faith hub at www.lindacureton.com.

www.ingramcontent.com/pod-product-compliance
Lightning Source LLC
Chambersburg PA
CBHW071732040426
42446CB00011B/2323